MW01103314

PACIFIC SALMON

Life Cycles

Jason Cooper

Rourke
Publishing LLC
Vero Beach, Florida 32964

www.rourkepublishing.com

PHOTO CREDITS: Cover, p. 4, 6, 7, 10, 16, 18, 19, 21, © Lynn M. Stone; p. 9, 11, 13, 15 © Brandon Cole.

Cover: *Fire engine red, sockeye salmon spawn in the shallow streams along the Adams River in British Columbia*

Editor: Frank Sloan

Cover and page design by Nicola Stratford

Library of Congress Cataloging-in-Publication Data

Cooper, Jason, 1942-
  Pacific salmon / Jason Cooper.
    p. cm. — (Life cycles)
Summary: Describes the physical characteristics, behavior, habitat, and life cycle of the Pacific salmon, with an emphasis on the hatching and growth of its young.
  ISBN 1-58952-352-0 (hardcover)
  1. Pacific salmon—Juvenile literature. [1. Pacific salmon. 2. Salmon.
3. Animals—Infancy.] I. Title.
  QL638.S2 C67 2002
  597.5'6--dc21

                                                                      2002006225

Printed in the USA

MP/W

Table of Contents

While spawning, salmon still have the energy to battle each other for nesting places.

Spawning Salmon

Pacific salmon have amazing life stories. Their stories begin in fresh water, but young salmon **migrate** to the ocean. They grow up in the sea. Then they migrate back to fresh water to **spawn**— and die.

Spawning fish lay eggs. Spawning creates a new generation of salmon to replace their parents.

Pacific Salmon of North America

Five kinds of Pacific salmon live in northwestern North America: coho, Chinook, pink, chum, and sockeye.

Sockeye salmon usually spawn only in streams that have lakes on their path.

Once silver, sockeyes turn fire engine red before they spawn and die.

Salmon spawn in cold, clear streams and rivers. The female uses her tail to dig a shallow nest, called a **redd**. Each pair of salmon may have four or five redds in the stream **gravel**.

Like pink pearls, salmon eggs lie on the gravel of a clean, clear stream in Canada.

Laying Eggs

A salmon lays thousands of soft, tiny eggs. The male salmon **fertilizes** them. That begins the growth of baby salmon inside the eggs.

Dead salmon add nutrients to the streams where they spawn.

Adding Nutrients

The salmon parents die shortly after spawning. But their rotting bodies are not wasted. Some of them feed big animals, like eagles and bears. But most salmon bodies rot in the stream. They add **nutrients** to the water. Nutrients are the good things that animals take into their bodies for food and growth.

Nutrients from dead salmon are food for tiny water animals. Those animals become food for baby salmon when they hatch. Through nature's design, the death of salmon parents helps baby salmon live!

From Egg to Adult

Salmon eggs **incubate** in the redd for several weeks or months. When the eggs hatch, the tiny salmon are called **alevins**. Each has a little bag called a yolk sac full of nutrients.

Alevins may take food from the yolk sacs on their bellies for several weeks.

The fry of sockeye, Chinook, and coho salmon live in fresh water.

By the time alevins are about 1 inch (2.5 centimeters) long, they have used up the yolk sac. The salmon, now called fry, leave the redd to find food. They eat insects and tiny, floating plants and animals. Meanwhile, the fry are prey for trout.

Pacific salmon grow at sea, with Chinooks often reaching weights of 30 or more pounds (14 kilograms).

Swimming to the Sea

Pink and chum fry immediately swim to sea. Sockeye, Chinook, and coho salmon fry live in fresh water for up to two years. At this stage of life they are known as **smolt**.

Pacific salmon may live at sea from six months to seven years. Some kinds become adults before others.

**These sockeyes are returning to their home stream, the
Adams River in British Columbia, Canada, to spawn.**

Returning Home

Most Pacific salmon live largely on smaller ocean fish. Sockeyes, however, eat small, floating plants and animals.

Adult salmon feel an urge to return to streams where they were born. Some salmon swim only about 150 miles (242 kilometers) from the sea to their home river. But others, especially some runs of Chinooks, migrate more than 2,500 miles (3,226 kilometers)!

Home to Fresh Water

Salmon enter fresh water where the streams pour into the sea. The journeys up spawning streams may be only a mile or two. But some fish travel several hundred miles.

Almost to its Alaskan spawning stream, a chum salmon hurls itself up a waterfall—and into the jaws of a brown bear.

Alaska brown bears learn early in life to catch salmon in their jaws, not with their paws.

The return to fresh water is filled with danger. Fishermen, bears, otters, and killer whales catch salmon. Dirty or heated water and water levels that are too high or too low are threats. Dams are also huge threats to salmon runs.

A sockeye salmon dies in the stream where it was born and spawned. Atlantic salmon spawn and return to the sea.

The Life Cycle Goes On

An adult Pacific salmon generally stops eating in fresh water. Its body changes shape and color. And as it spawns, the strength that has brought it on this incredible journey flows away. Its life's journey soon ends—at almost exactly the same place where it began.

Stage 1: Pacific salmon lay their eggs in nests in fresh water.

Stage 4: Pacific salmon return to fresh water to lay their eggs.

Stage 2: Salmon incubate their eggs until they hatch.

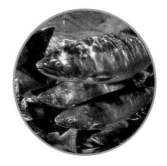

Stage 3: When some Pacific salmon are grown, they leave fresh water and live in the sea.

Glossary

alevins (AL eh venz) — newly hatched salmon with their yolk sac attached

fertilizes (FUR tuh lie zez) — to make an egg, such as a salmon's, develop and grow into an animal

gravel (GRAV uhl) — loose, rounded bits of rock

incubate (INK you bait) — to keep eggs warm; to develop and grow within an egg

migrate (MY grait) — to make a long, seasonal journey at the same time each year

nutrients (NEW tree entz) — things that animals take into their bodies for food and growth

redd (RED) — the gravel nest of salmon in a stream

smolt (SMOLT) — a young salmon as it gains its silvery, adult color

spawn (SPAHN) — to lay eggs in water

Index

Further Reading

Hirschi, Ron. *Salmon.* Lerner, 2000

Reed-Jones, Carol. *Salmon Stream.* Dawn Publications, 2001

Websites to Visit

http://search.yahooligans.com/search/ligans?p=pacific+salmon

http://www.cf.adfg.state.ak.us/geninfo/research/genetics/kids/spawning.htm

About the Author

Jason Cooper has written several children's books about a variety of topics for Rourke Publishing, including recent series *China Discovery* and *American Landmarks*. Cooper travels widely to gather information for his books. Two of his favorite travel destinations are Alaska and the Far East.